Brilliant Activities for

Grammar and Punctuation, Year 6

Activities for Developing and Reinforcing Key Language Skills

Irene Yates

Brilliant
PUBLICATIONS

This set of books is dedicated to the memory of Miss Hannah Gamage and to the children of St. Philip Neri with St. Bede's Catholic Primary School, Mansfield.

• •

We hope you and your pupils enjoy using the ideas in this book. Brilliant Publications publishes many other books to help primary school teachers. To find out more details on all of our titles, including those listed below, please log onto our website. www.brilliantpublications.co.uk.

Other books in the Brilliant Activities for Grammar and Punctuation Series

	Printed ISBN	e-pdf ISBN
Year 1	978-1-78317-125-5	978-1-78317-132-3
Year 2	978-1-78317-126-2	978-1-78317-133-0
Year 3	978-1-78317-127-9	978-1-78317-134-7
Year 4	978-1-78317-128-6	978-1-78317-135-4
Year 5	978-1-78317-129-3	978-1-78317-136-1

Brilliant Activities for Creative Writing Series

Year 1	978-0-85747-463-6
Year 2	978-0-85747-464-3
Year 3	978-0-85747-465-0
Year 4	978-0-85747-466-7
Year 5	978-0-85747-467-4
Year 6	978-0-85747-468-1

Brilliant Activities for Reading Comprehension Series

Year 1	978-1-78317-070-8
Year 2	978-1-78317-071-5
Year 3	978-1-78317-072-2
Year 4	978-1-78317-073-9
Year 5	978-1-78317-074-6
Year 6	978-1-78317-075-3

Published by Brilliant Publications
Unit 10
Sparrow Hall Farm
Edlesborough
Dunstable
Bedfordshire
LU6 2ES, UK

Email:	info@brilliantpublications.co.uk
Website:	www.brilliantpublications.co.uk
Tel:	01525 222292

The name Brilliant Publications and the logo are registered trademarks.

Written by Irene Yates
Illustrated by Molly Sage
Front cover illustration by Molly Sage

© Text Irene Yates 2016
© Design Brilliant Publications 2016

Printed ISBN 978-1-78317-130-9
e-pdf ISBN 978-1-78317-137-8

First printed and published in the UK in 2016

Contents

Introduction

The **Brilliant Activities for Grammar and Punctuation** series is designed to introduce and reinforce grammatical concepts in line with the National Curriculum Programmes of Study.

The rules of Grammar and Punctuation are not always easy to access and absorb – or even to teach. It is difficult for children to make the leap from speaking and writing to talking about speaking and writing and to think in the abstract about the words of the language. The ability or readiness to do this requires a certain way of thinking and, for the most part, repetition is the key.

The sheets for this series are all written to add to the children's understanding of these fairly abstract ideas. They aim to improve children's ability to use English effectively and accurately in their own writing and speaking.

The sheets contain oral as well as written contexts because Grammar and Punctuation are not just about writing. Sometimes the way children have learned to speak is not always grammatically correct but it is the way of speaking that they own. We always have to be aware of instances of regional or familial language and make the point that what we are teaching is what is known universally as 'correct' speech without deprecating the children's own patterns of speech.

The children should always be encouraged to discuss what it is they are learning, to ask questions and to make observations. All of this discussion will help them to understand how the English language works.

The sheets are designed to be structured but flexible so that they can be used to introduce a concept, as stand-alones or as follow-ons. The activities on the sheets can be used as templates to create lots more for practice and reinforcement purposes.

Each book aims to offer:
* groundwork for the introduction of new concepts
* a range of relevant activities
* ideas for continuation
* opportunity for reinforcement
* simple and clear definition of concepts and terms
* opportunities for assessing learning
* clear information for teachers.

Grammar and Punctuation can sometimes be a hard grind, but nothing feels so good to a teacher as a pupil, eyes shining, saying, 'Oh, I get that now!' Once they 'get' a concept they never lose it and you can watch it become functional in their writing and, hopefully, hear it become functional in their speaking.

Links to the curriculum

The activity sheets in this series of books will help children to develop their knowledge of Grammar and Punctuation as set out in the Programmes of Study and Appendix 2 of the 2014 National Curriculum for England.

Each book focuses on the concepts to be introduced during that relevant year. Where appropriate, content from previous years is revisited to consolidate knowledge and build on children's understanding.

What's the difference?

What's the difference between:

a man eating strawberry   and   a man-eating strawberry

Answer: a hyphen!

Hyphens avoid ambiguity – they save confusion.

Draw cartoons to show the difference between:

a walking-stick and a walking stick	a frog-jumping contest and a frog jumping contest
an alien-spotting boy and an alien spotting boy	a grandma-spooking spider and a grandma spooking spider

Create three 'hyphen' cartoons of your own.

> ## Make up as many weird hyphenated combinations as you can in five minutes.

Point out that hyphens join two words together. There should be no spaces either side of a hyphen.

Brilliant Activities for Grammar and Punctuation, Year 6
© Irene Yates and Brilliant Publications

Dot dot dot ...

The punctuation mark ... is called an ellipsis.

You can use it to show that:

◆ something is missed out, like this:
Once upon a time ... and they all lived happily ever after.

◆ to show something is continued, like this:
There were hundreds of vegetables – carrots, cabbages, potatoes, peas ...

◆ to add tension for your reader, like this:
Ayesha opened the door and then ... whoosh! Out jumped a black cat.

Talk with your partner to make up three sentences for each of the three ways ellipses can be used. Write them here.

_____

_____

_____

_____

_____

_____

_____

_____

_____

_____

> **Have fun making up sentences where the ellipsis adds tension. You start a sentence ending 'dot, dot, dot'. Your partner has to complete it. Swap.**

Scan through shared texts together to find examples of ellipses and discuss why they are there.

What's a colon?

My favourite games are: hide and seek, darts, anti-litter.

A colon is a punctuation mark, made up of two dots like this :

It introduces more information:

Notice that you still need to remember to put commas between items in the lists.

These are my favourite foods: chips, broccoli, apple, fish.

You will need to bring with you: pens, pencils, scrapbooks, scissors.

Write out six sentences of your own, using a colon.

_____

_____

_____

_____

_____

_____

_____

_____

_____

> **Make up a sandwich recipe together, using colons for sections on what you need and what you do.**

Have the children look through reference books in pairs to find examples and share them with the class.

Brilliant Activities for Grammar and Punctuation, Year 6
© Irene Yates and Brilliant Publications

And a semi-colon is ...

A semi-colon is made up of a dot and a comma, like this ; .

It is used instead of a conjunction to join two short sentences, like this:

> It was nearly Christmas; we searched for our presents.

Take out the conjunction and put a semi-colon into these sentences:

He was tired out because he'd never run so fast.

_____

My teacher is good but I have to listen carefully.

_____

We play football in winter and we play cricket in summer.

_____

She wanted to visit her nan but she had no bus fare.

_____

Talk about, compose and write four semi-colon sentences of your own.

_____

_____

_____

_____

With a partner discuss which conjunctions could be used instead of the semi-colon in the sentences you have written.

Talk about how colons differ from semi-colons. Set the children off on a semi-colon hunt in their reading books; share and display.

Watch that bullet point!

Bullet points can highlight the more important parts of a text, or they can take the place of commas in a list, like this:

The rules say:
- [ ] no running in the corridors
- [ ] show respect to everyone
- [ ] be considerate
- [ ] no phones in school

The recipe needs:
- milk
- eggs
- flour
- cheese

Make up bullet point lists for:

My friends and family

Endangered species

With your partner, look around the classroom. Can you see any examples of lists using bullet points?

Look for examples of bullet point lists in reference books. Note that sometimes bullet-pointed lists are punctuated with commas or semi-colons. This is a matter of 'house style'. Look for examples with and without punctuation.

Brilliant Activities for Grammar and Punctuation, Year 6
© Irene Yates and Brilliant Publications

More semi-colons

You can use semi-colons to separate complex lists, like this:

At the café we had toast with marmalade; bacon and eggs and mushrooms; freshly squeezed orange juice.

Put semi-colons into these sentences:

For the trip, Emma has brought her rucksack full of games to play two sets of pyjamas her mum's photograph six different kinds of biscuit a teddy bear with only one eye.

In the dressing-up box were hats of all kinds and shapes jackets with buttons and zips so many shoes you wouldn't believe masks of every animal you can think of enough tops and trousers for the whole class.

Write sentences with semi-colon lists beginning:

At the seaside _____

_____

At the safari park _____

_____

In the morning _____

_____

_____

> **With your partner, create a paragraph for an adventure story which uses a sentence structured like this, about building a shelter on a treasure island.**

Practise making up complex lists verbally, before pupils write out their own sentences using semi-colon lists.

Bullet points with semi-colons

Sometimes bullet-pointed lists use semi-colons after each item, like this:

Parts of speech:
- nouns – naming words;
- pronouns – use instead of nouns;
- adjectives – describing words;
- verbs – action and being words;
- adverbs – telling how things are done;
- prepositions – show place;
- conjunctions – joining words.

Notice how the first word in each bullet starts with a lower case or small letter and the last mark is a full stop.

Make a list like this for all the punctuation marks you know.

_____

_____

_____

_____

_____

_____

_____

_____

_____

_____

_____

Look in reference books together to find examples of semi-colons used in lists.

The choice of using semi-colons, commas or no punctuation is usually a 'house style', which the publisher has chosen. It has to be consistent throughout a magazine, book or other publication.

Brilliant Activities for Grammar and Punctuation, Year 5
© Irene Yates and Brilliant Publications

A semi-colon's job is never done

Another way of using a semi-colon is to use it instead of a dash, to join two independent clauses, like this:

The rain was pelting down; it was raining cats and dogs!

My dad's always laughing; my dad's cool.

I hate shopping; supermarkets bore me.

Remember – an independent clause makes total sense on its own.

Write six examples, using a semi-colon, here;

_____

_____

_____

_____

_____

_____

One partner says a short independent clause. The other 'writes' a semi-colon in the air and adds another short independent clause to finish the sentence. Swap.

Explain what is meant by 'house style'. Every publication has its own 'house style'. Look at newspapers and magazines to find ways they can be different.

Using a dash

 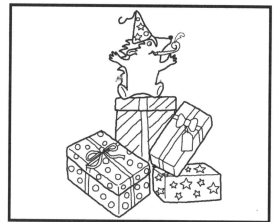

A **dash** (–) has a space each side of it (unlike a hyphen which doesn't). You can use a dash to join two independent clauses together. Like this:

It's my birthday – I'm happy.

Jack batted the ball – Jess caught it.

> Remember – an independent clause makes total sense on its own.

We went to a theme park – it was a great day out.

Write six sentences using dashes here:

_____

_____

_____

_____

_____

_____

_____

_____

_____

Say a short sentence (independent clause). You partner needs to do a hand motion to indicate a dash and then complete the sentence with another independent clause. Swap. Try to make the sentence funny.

Talk about the difference between a hyphen and a dash. Show how dashes can be used in sentences to provide emphasis.

Brilliant Activities for Grammar and Punctuation, Year 6
© Irene Yates and Brilliant Publications

Colons can work, too

When it comes to independent clauses, you can choose to join them with either a dash, a semi-colon or a colon. Use a colon likes this:

The sausages for tea have disappeared: the dog has a guilty look!

It's a freezing cold day: there's frost on the hill.

I went skateboarding yesterday: I broke my leg!

Finish off these sentences with a colon and another independent clause.

Remember, the two clauses must relate closely to each other.

The table was overflowing with food

_____

The farmer surveyed his newly planted field

_____

The bus stop is two blocks away

_____

The clown threw the juggling balls in the air

_____

Write two sentences of your own, using a colon to join independent clauses.

_____

_____

_____

_____

Make up some jokes that might need to be punctuated with colons. For example: This cat lives in the sea: it's an octopus!

Talk about the different ways to join independent clauses. Colons are often used so that the second sentence summarises, sharpens or explains the first. Which pair can make the funniest sentence?

And the subject is ...

In a sentence, a verb has a 'subject'. The subject is the noun or pronoun that is doing (being/feeling/having) the action of the verb. Like this:

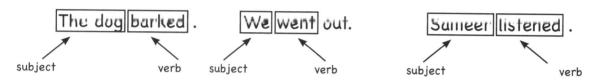

The dog barked .

subject   verb

We went out.

subject   verb

Sameer listened .

subject   verb

Read these subjects and add a verb:

A snake   <u>slithers.</u>

A horse _____

A duck _____

A bird _____

A mouse _____

A lion _____

A butterfly _____

A hen _____

We _____

You _____

They _____

Make up funny sentences: take it in turns to choose a subject and your partner concludes the sentence, eg 'Custard nests in trees'.

Use a shared text to pick out the subjects and the verbs, giving every child an opportunity to have a turn.

Brilliant Activities for Grammar and Punctuation, Year 6
© Irene Yates and Brilliant Publications

And the object is ...

We know that, in a sentence, a verb has a 'subject'.

It may also have an 'object'. The object is the 'receiver' of the verb. Like this:

The dog	barked	at	the postman
subject	verb		object

We	went	to	the park
subject	verb		object

Add subjects and verbs to these objects, to form sentences.

Water pours out of _____ the tap.

_____ a mouse.

_____ trees.

_____ dinosaurs.

_____ jokes.

_____ thunder.

_____ leaf.

_____ garden.

_____ the page.

_____ the table.

What do you get if you cross a dog with a lion?

A terrified postman! Ha ha.

In threes, make up funny sentences with a subject, a verb and an object. First pupil calls out a subject, eg 'Bill', second pupil calls out a verb, eg 'ate', and the third pupil calls out an object, eg 'the lion'.

Use a shared text for the children to take turns in identifying subjects, verbs and objects.

The order of words

Look at the order of the words in these sentences:

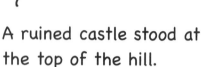
A ruined castle stood at the top of the hill.

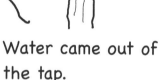
Water came out of the tap.

The dog chewed on the bone.

In each sentence the 'subject' comes at the beginning. The way these sentences are written, with the subject first, is called the **active voice**.

Write six sentences of your own in the active voice. Illustrate one.

_____

_____

_____

_____

_____

_____

_____

_____

_____

┌─ **Verbalise your sentences with your partner before you start to write. Check that the subject comes first.** ─┐

Look for examples of the active voice in shared texts.

Brilliant Activities for Grammar and Punctuation, Year 6
© Irene Yates and Brilliant Publications

Changing the order

You can add variety to your writing by changing the order of the words in a sentence. You can put the 'subject' last, like this.

At the top of the hill [stood] a [ruined castle].
              verb   subject

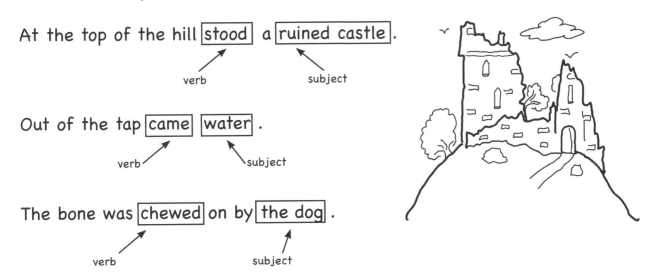

Out of the tap [came] [water].
        verb   subject

The bone was [chewed] on by [the dog].
        verb   subject

Remember that the 'subject' is always the noun or pronoun that does the action. The way these sentences are written, with the subject last, is called the **passive voice.**

Write six sentences of your own in the passive voice.

_____

_____

_____

_____

_____

_____

> **Verbalise your sentences with your partner before you start to write. Check that the subject comes last.**

Play 'Spot the passive voice sentences' using shared texts. Talk about how the feeling of a piece changes when the voice changes from active to passive. Encourage pupils to experiment with changing the voice in their writing.

Verb voice

A verb can be in the active or the passive voice. The voice of the verb tells whether the subject is doing the action (active voice), or whether something is being done to the subject (passive voice).

When the passive voice is used the verb may change a bit and a helping verb is added. In the following example, the verb changes from 'read' to 'was read':

Active voice: Gemma **read** the book.
Passive voice: The book **was read** by Gemma.

Make these sentences more direct by changing them into the active voice:

A big, hairy spider was pounced on by my dog.

_____

The activities are all chosen by the children in the group.

_____

The flowers were all picked by my Nan.

_____

Six goals were scored by Henry.

_____

The cat was frightened by the frog.

_____

Ten stickers were awarded to Kevin.

_____

> **Talk about the two voices of each sentence. Decide which you think sounds or reads better. Discuss why.**

Have children act out an action. Describe it in an active and passive voice. Talk about when it would be good to use the active voice and when a passive voice might be better.

Brilliant Activities for Grammar and Punctuation, Year 6
© Irene Yates and Brilliant Publications

Verb voice again

A verb can be in the active or the passive voice. The voice of the verb tells whether the subject is doing the action (active voice), or whether something is being done to the subject (passive voice).

Make these sentences less direct by changing them from the active voice into the passive voice, like this:

Active voice: Ryan wore the owl mask.

Passive voice: The owl mask was worn by Ryan.

Tony fixed the car.

_____

Rain stopped the carnival parade.

_____

The noise came from under a bush.

_____

Humpty Dumpty fell off the wall.

_____

The chicken walked across the road.

_____

Jenna stood by the table.

_____

The dog gobbled up the sausages.

_____

The aliens stepped out of the UFO.

_____

The squirrel ran across the fence.

_____

> **Talk about the two voices of each sentence. Decide which you think sounds or reads better. Discuss why.**

Have children act out an action. Describe it in an active and passive voice. Discuss what difference it could make to their writing.

Words with more than one meaning

Some words have more than one meaning, like this:

I bought **stamps** for my letters.
Josh **stamps** his foot.

We went by **train** to town.
My Dad has to **train** to be a fireman.

Can you write two sentences for each of these words? (Use a dictionary if you need help.)

check	hide	lock	sound
swallow	spoke	trunk	light

_____

_____

_____

_____

_____

_____

_____

_____

Together, look up the words you don't know. Think of four more you could add to this list.

Talk and get suggestions for more words with more than one meaning. Make a display with example sentences. See also Homographs (page 37).

Brilliant Activities for Grammar and Punctuation, Year 5
© Irene Yates and Brilliant Publications

Words that help your writing

There are lots of words we use in talking or exchanging texts with our friends which we would change for more formal words if we were talking to, or writing to, other people.

Read the words on the top row.

try	stop	ask	make	buy
attempt	cease	inquire	manufacture	purchase

We can exchange them for words that are similar, but more formal in meaning, like the words underneath.

Draw lines to link these words:

scared	regret
annual	damp
sorry	round
sleepy	brave
reply	frightened
moist	drowsy
circular	answer
courageous	yearly

Write a text to a friend using some of these words.

Write a letter to a school governor, using more formal words.

Think of words you use all the time when talking and writing that you might find more formal words for. Find at least ten between you.

Discuss using more formality in writing. When and why would the children use informality and formality? Use one of their ideas to draft examples together.

Base words

A **base word** is a word from which other words can be built by adding a prefix and/or a suffix. Like this:

reason + un + able = **un**reason**able**

want + un + ed = **un**want**ed**

Add a prefix and a suffix to each of these base words:

appear ——————————————   respect ——————————————

correct——————————————   honest ——————————————

certain ——————————————   pleasant ——————————————

construct——————————————   joy ——————————————

Find the base words of these words:

	Base word	Prefix	Suffix
unemployment			
uncertainty			
disrespectful			
reconstruction			
unpleasantness			
dishonourable			
imprisonment			
enjoyable			
informally			
incorrectly			
reappearing			

With a partner find 10 more words of your own.

Organise a word collection display board of base words with prefixes and suffixes they might take.

Brilliant Activities for Grammar and Punctuation, Year 6
© Irene Yates and Brilliant Publications

Compound words

Compound words are made up of two
or more smaller words. Like this:

earth + quake = earthquake

note + book = notebook

These compound words have got all muddled up. Can you sort them out?

cheesebrow everyache homeball

footshake   handfly   toothwork

eyeburger   butterday

1. _____ 5. _____

2. _____ 6. _____

3. _____ 7. _____

4. _____ 8. _____

Find eight compound words of your own. Muddle them up. Get your friend
to sort them out.

1. _____ 5. _____

2. _____ 6. _____

3. _____ 7. _____

4. _____ 8. _____

> **Together, work out five compound words that join two nouns,
> eg shell + fish = shellfish. Then work out five compound words that
> join an adjective and a noun, eg black + bird = blackbird.**

Challenge the children to write down as many compound words as they can in 10 minutes.

Does it mean the same?

A **synonym** is a word that has a
similar meaning to another word,
like this:

strange = odd
unusual = peculiar

get = obtain = achieve = acquire

The words don't mean **exactly** the same but they have shades of the same
meaning so that when you write you need to try to find the most appropriate
word for that piece of writing.

Find as many synonyms as you can for these words:

coast _____

daring _____

jump _____

honest _____

hot _____

good _____

Take one of your words. Write two different sentences, using synonyms to
make the vocabulary appropriate to the situation.

_____

_____

_____

_____

> **Writers choose their words very carefully! Take the sentence, 'Jack
> went out of the classroom'. How many different ways of saying 'went'
> can you think of? For example: rushed, ran, climbed ...**

*Help the children to choose their words carefully. Demonstrate how writers give a different 'tone' to a sentence by such
word choice, using their discussion of synonyms for 'went' as a focus.*

Brilliant Activities for Grammar and Punctuation, Year 6
© Irene Yates and Brilliant Publications

Synonym word search

Find all the words in the grid. Write each one beside its synonym in the list.

f	l	a	v	o	u	r	d	e	p
s	a	b	e	c	l	x	p	m	e
n	r	d	l	l	a	d	t	t	c
r	g	s	i	c	k	a	i	i	l
g	e	a	p	p	u	o	n	p	a
e	m	p	t	y	c	f	y	u	p
x	f	l	a	o	s	t	i	g	n
y	e	x	i	t	o	u	b	x	s
e	m	p	s	t	r	a	n	g	e

List:

big _____

small _____

taste _____

ill _____

odd _____

ancient _____

mend _____

hollow _____

applaud _____

way out _____

You can learn hundreds of new words by looking up synonyms. Work out as many new words as you can to exchange for the word 'said'. Make a chart or word search of them.

Introduce children to a dictionary of synonyms and antonyms. Explore its use as an aid to developing their vocabulary and writing.

Does it mean the opposite?

An **antonym** is a word that has the opposite
meaning to another word. Like this:

    present – absent
    hollow   – solid
    heavy   – light

Write examples of **antonyms** for these words:

storm _____

_____

quick _____

_____

hurry _____

_____

silence _____

_____

enormous _____

_____

entertain _____

_____

entrance _____

_____

enter _____

_____

universal _____

_____

tidiness _____

_____

> **In pairs, give each other words and find antonyms. How many
> pairs of words can you write down in five minutes?**

*Children could use a thesaurus to help, but encourage them to try to think of words on their own first, then use the
thesaurus as an extension activity.*

Brilliant Activities for Grammar and Punctuation, Year 6
© Irene Yates and Brilliant Publications

Antonym word search

Find all the words in the grid. Write each one beside its antonym in the list.

f	s	m	i	l	e	c	r	t	i
o	m	t	q	u	t	r	o	i	m
f	q	u	i	e	t	y	g	l	e
a	t	h	e	g	c	j	o	m	d
k	y	q	u	o	h	y	g	e	u
e	n	o	i	f	e	t	h	a	e
t	i	m	i	d	a	s	e	n	a
b	r	a	c	k	p	v	y	l	u
e	x	p	e	l	i	g	h	t	h

List:

hot _____

loose _____

real _____

generous _____

laugh _____

expensive _____

heavy _____

noisy _____

frown _____

brave _____

Together, make up your own dictionary of useful synonyms and antonyms to use when you are writing.

Use a dictionary of synonyms and antonyms. Call out a word. Children find a possible antonym.

The modal verbs

The **modal verbs** are:

can	could	would	will	shall
should	must	might	may	

These verbs aren't like ordinary verbs because they can't change their form (eg by adding 's' or 'ed') and they always have another verb with them. Like this:

Karen said, 'I (shall) have a baked potato.'

(Can) you get some shopping for me?

I (might) go to town tomorrow.

} The modal verbs are circled.

Write 10 sentences of your own using the modal verbs and underline them. Try to write five statement sentences and five question sentences.

_____

_____

_____

_____

_____

_____

_____

_____

_____

_____

Discuss the difference between 'You may tidy your room', 'You should tidy your room' and 'You must tidy your room'.

Look for modal verbs in a shared text, together.

Brilliant Activities for Grammar and Punctuation, Year 6
© Irene Yates and Brilliant Publications

More about modal verbs ...

Sometimes you hear people say things like 'I could <u>of</u> done it'; 'I would <u>of</u> done it'; 'I might <u>of</u> been there.' Sometimes they even write it down this way.

They are so wrong! Do you know why?

It is because what they really mean to use is a modal verb with a contraction of 'have', like this:

I could've (could have) done it.

I would've (would have) done it.

I might've (might have) done it.

You already know about contractions. Now you know about modal verbs, so put the two together. Tell everybody else how wrong they are!

Write 10 sentences using the modal verbs and the contraction of 'have' – ''ve'.

_____

_____

_____

_____

_____

_____

_____

_____

_____

Listen to yourselves chatting. How often do you find yourself saying 'of' instead of 'have'? How often do you write it by mistake? Look back at some of your work to find out.

Make a display banning the use of 'of' with modal verbs and showing the contraction of 'have'.

Negative modal verbs

You can make modal verbs negative by adding 'not' or the contraction 'n't', like this:

I must not (mustn't) forget my PE kit.

I cannot (can't) find my trainers.

Make these sentences into negatives; use contractions for some of them:

You might be lucky and win. _____

She would believe me. _____

I could eat an elephant. _____

I should be late for school. _____

They will catch cold in the rain. (Watch out!)

_____

He might be on time. _____

I may watch the programme. _____

They must hurry. _____

They can dance and sing. _____

Turn these into positives:

I shan't be there. _____

I shouldn't have bothered. _____

She mightn't be early. _____

He won't like it. _____

Make up a section of dialogue for a play together. Use two characters talking and give each one two negative modal verbs.

Find a piece of shared text that can be changed by using modal verbs and do it all together, modelling what you do.

Brilliant Activities for Grammar and Punctuation, Year 6
© Irene Yates and Brilliant Publications

The subjunctive

The subjunctive mood is a very formal style of writing and speaking. Using subjunctive verbs is like saying something is not really true. Like this:

Ordinary verb: I'm going to town so I'll take you.

Subjunctive verb: If I <u>were</u> going to town I'd take you (but I'm not).

Ordinary verb: I'm rich so you can have whatever you like.

Subjunctive verb: If I <u>were</u> rich you could have whatever you like (but I'm not).

Write subjunctive sentences using 'were' for these. You will have to alter the words quite a bit.

If it rains we'll postpone the match.

_____

When wishes and dreams come true you'll be OK.

_____

Wild cats are as tame as domestic cats – they're safe.

_____

Your dog is trained properly so I'll let it in.

_____

Those children are well behaved so I'll enjoy being with them.

_____

Grandad wears a hat to keep his head warm.

_____

> **With a partner make up a poem about winning lots of money.**
> **Start each line: If I were to...**

The subjunctive mood is rarely used in contemporary texts, but pupils may encounter it when reading older classics. Pupils should be aware of it.

The present perfect tense

The present perfect tense of a verb shows us that something started in the past but is still going on. Like this:

The dog has barked all night.
The boys have played outside all day.

These sentences suggest that the dog is still barking and that the boys are still playing outside.

The present perfect tense always uses '**has**' or '**have**'. If you said, "The dog barked all night," you would be saying it had stopped barking now.

Write present perfect verbs to change these sentences:

1. Yasmin <u>went</u> to the shops.

2. Billy <u>sang</u> in the choir.

3. The boys baked for the fair.

4. The girls practised high jump.

Write four of your own.

_____

_____

_____

_____

_____

_____

_____

> **Talk together in a group and see if you can spot each other's present perfect verbs.**

Talk about how the present perfect continuous tense is formed, for example, the dog has been barking all night.

Brilliant Activities for Grammar and Punctuation, Year 6
© Irene Yates and Brilliant Publications

Formal language

Formal language which is used in official letters and on public signs doesn't sound quite the same as everyday English because it is impersonal and often leaves out pronouns and contractions.

NO LITTER.

Everyday English: Don't drop your litter here.
Official English: No litter.

Everyday English: Dogs shouldn't be walked here.
Official English: Dogs prohibited.

Write in your workbook everyday English sentences for these formal and/or official ones.

No bicycles on this path.

DANGER
Swimming
prohibited.

Dogs on leads only.

Send entries to the address above.

It has been brought to our attention that you wish to leave the school.

Visitors are requested to refrain from touching the exhibits.

Think and talk about official/formal language that you see all the time but have probably never paid any attention to before.

With children, work out which rules they might apply to official writing. Create some rules for the classroom/playground in everyday language, then rewrite them using official language. Which are the children most happy with. Why?

Improve your layout

The way you organise the text on the page can make a big difference to how easy it is to read.

Draw lines to show where these devices are used in the example.

Heading

Subheadings

Columns

Bullets

Tables

NEW PLAYGROUND OPENS

HEADTEACHER OPENS PLAYGROUND

Mrs Bigtoes, the headteacher at Markton Primary School officially opened the new playground this afternoon.

The new playground has:
* swings
* slides
* climbing frame
* quiet areas
* football goals
* tree house

JOINT FUND-RAISING EFFORT

Money for the playground came from a variety of sources.

Friends of Markton School	£10,000
School funds	£10,000
Anonymous local business woman	£20,000

In her speech Mrs Bigtoes praised the fund-raising efforts of the parents and thanked the anonymous local business woman for her very generous donation.

Pick a topic that is of concern to you. Write an article about it using as many of these devices as you can. Plan your article here.

Think up a piece of classroom news together. Plan how you could present it as a poster using these ideas.

Use shared texts to find how headings, subheadings, columns, bullets and tables can be used to make meaning clearer. Encourage pupils to use these features in their information writing.

Homographs

A **homograph** is a word with the same spelling as another but with a different meaning. Like this:

palm: I had a spider in the **palm** of my hand.   The **palm** trees were gusting in the wind.

What did the hurricane say to the palm tree?

Hang on to your leaves, I'm no ordinary breeze!

Talk about the meanings for these words. Write two sentences for each homograph, making sure the different meanings of the words are clear.

seal _____

_____

well _____

_____

kind _____

_____

pupil _____

_____

stone _____

_____

safe _____

_____

fire _____

_____

calf _____

_____

You need to be sure of your spellings to recognise homographs. Together, think up six, check in a dictionary to see if you are right.

Challenge time! How many homographs can the group suggest in ten minutes? Write them down, so they can check.

Homophones

A homophone is a word with the same sound as another, but with a different spelling and meaning. Like this:

guessed
I guessed we'd have a great day.

guest
Our guest writer was in school today.

Write a sentence for each word, making their meanings clear, like the examples given above.

male _____

mail _____

waste _____

waist _____

meddle _____

medal _____

vein _____

vain _____

boys _____

buoys _____

sum _____

some _____

berry _____

bury _____

witch _____

which _____

How many pairs of words that are homophones can you think of – excluding those above – in five minutes? Can you think of any triples?

Collect all the pairs of homophones and make a display of them.

Brilliant Activities for Grammar and Punctuation, Year 6
© Irene Yates and Brilliant Publications

Homonyms

Which group of homonyms do these words belong to? Pair them up and write the pairs in the correct column in the table.

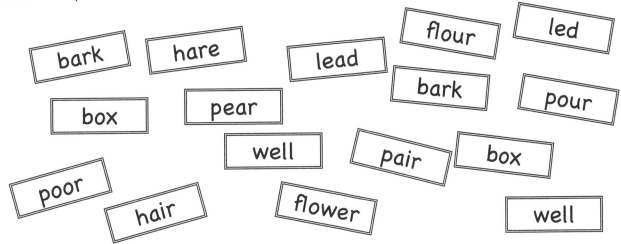

Homographs	Homophones

With a partner, think of as many homonyms as you can in 10 minutes.

Make a list of words. Challenge the children to find corresponding homonyms and decide which set they belong to.

Don't do this!

You know how to make a sentence negative, like this:

I didn't see anything.

What you **must not** do is put in two negatives, like this:

I didn't see nothing.

Because, if you didn't see nothing, you must have seen something! Two negatives turn into a positive and confuse the issue.

Negative words
not   ...n't   nothing   nowhere   nobody   no   none   never

Change these double-negative sentences into straightforward negative ones:

She didn't want nothing. _____

They couldn't play no games. _____

There wasn't none left. _____

That old man doesn't like nobody. _____

We never went nowhere. _____

She don't want no sandwiches. _____

He doesn't know nothing. _____

We've never had none of these games. _____

_____

> **Take turns to make up a double negative sentence using 'nowhere', 'nobody', or 'nothing'. Your partner has to make the sentence positive.**

Have a verbal game, turning positive sentences into negative sentences, then into double negatives meaning the same as the first sentence.

Brilliant Activities for Grammar and Punctuation, Year 6
© Irene Yates and Brilliant Publications

Anagrams

An anagram is a word from which the letters can be rearranged to form a different word.
Like this:

ogre   =   gore   =   goer =   ergo
broad   =   board
melon   =   lemon

Rearrange these words to make new ones:

seal _____

plum _____

rose _____

mane _____

rats _____

last _____

mate _____

same _____

verse _____

garden _____

Sometimes it helps to break anagrams down and put the letters into alphabetical order, like this:

petal   =   aelpt   =   plate

Can you work out which words these make?

aals _____   aenprrt _____

abdn _____   aenprtt _____

achir _____   aaccdeim _____

achls _____   aaccertu _____

aadfir _____   aadlns _____

Get children to put letters of words into alphabetical order and test each other. Use a timer to make a competitive game.

Similes

A simile is a 'figure of speech' that compares one thing with another, like this:

as cold as ice

as warm as toast

When something is very light we say it is 'as light as a feather' because it is similar to a feather in weight.

How many of these well-known similes do you know?

as cunning as a __ __ __

as proud as a __ __ __ __ __ __ __

as flat as a __ __ __ __ __ __ __

as old as the __ __ __ __ __ __

as fresh as a __ __ __ __ __

as safe as __ __ __ __ __ __

as quick as __ __ __ __ __ __ __ __ __

as sweet as __ __ __ __ __

as black as __ __ __ __

as busy as a __ __ __

Make up some similes of your own here:

as wet as _____

as big as _____

as strong as _____

as gentle as _____

as graceful as _____

Compare your words with a friend.

See how many well-known similes the children can find.

Brilliant Activities for Grammar and Punctuation, Year 6
© Irene Yates and Brilliant Publications

Metaphors

Metaphors are 'figures of speech' that imply or suppose that one thing is another.

We use metaphors in our speech all the time like this.

She's got her head in the clouds.

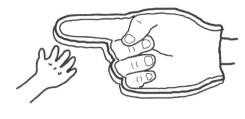

Give me a hand.

Pick your feet up!

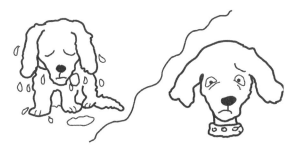

Don't be so wet!

Make up two sentences for each of these words – one sentence with a literal (real) meaning and one with a metaphorical meaning.

snail _____

_____

river _____

_____

universe_____

_____

forest _____

_____

Discuss any sentences or phrases that you have heard that are really metaphors: 'He's a football nut.'

Use shared texts to find similes and metaphors and compare them. Have lots of talking and discussion. Encourage pupils to use similes and metaphors in their writing.

Rhyming words

Words that rhyme are words that end with the same sound, like this:

sound / bound / round / ground / found

Find as many words as you can that rhyme with:

howl	heal	load	shout	beat
beam	rain	bite	late	share

Make up an eight-line poem using some of the words. Have the lines rhyme in two different ways. Choose which you feel works best.

A _____   A _____
A _____   B _____
B _____   A _____
B _____   B _____
C _____   C _____
C _____   D _____
D _____   C _____
D _____   D _____

Use different words if you need to.

With a partner look at the rhymes you have each found. Together can you think of any more?

Start to construct a class rhyming dictionary. The children can refer to it and also add to it whenever they are writing. Model the two different rhyme formats given, if necessary.

Brilliant Activities for Grammar and Punctuation, Year 6
© Irene Yates and Brilliant Publications

A linking device

When you are writing, you know that each paragraph must lead on to the next one in some way and that they have to have some kind of connection.

There are ways that writers have, called 'devices', that help you to do this.

One way is to repeat a word, like this:

> Samuel peered through a grimy window of the old cottage into the darkened room. Through the grime and dirt, he could see the sparsely furnished room; it contained a single bed, a wooden crate for a table. The room looked empty, but then peering again, he could just about make out the silhouette of a women cradling a baby, when the front door opened suddenly - it was the man!
>
> The man was ...

Write two paragraphs about a subject of your choice. End the first and begin the second with the same words.

_____

_____

_____

_____

_____

_____

_____

_____

_____

Together, have a look at a piece of fiction and try to work out how the paragraphs are linked.

Show how the children can use the same technique, using ellipses instead of words.

Alphabet fun

Work through the alphabet to find:

1. Words that <u>begin</u> and <u>end</u> with the same letter, like this:

    arena, blob, colic,

2. Words that will make up a sentence of up to 10 words, in which each word begins with the same letter. For example:

    Beautiful barefoot ballerinas balance bravely blindfolded between bright bronze beams.

or

    Eleven enormous entertaining elephants entered Europe's electrifyingly exciting emporium.

How many letters of the alphabet can you do this for?

3. Use words that you can advertise or describe yourself with, beginning with the letter **a** and going through to **z**, like this:

    agreeable, beautiful, cool ...

Use dictionaries and thesauruses for these exercises.

Brilliant Activities for Grammar and Punctuation, Year 6
© Irene Yates and Brilliant Publications

Quiz 1

What kind of word am I?

Add at least 20 words to each box.

Clue: C _ _ _ _ _ _ N _ _ _	Clue: A _ _ _ _ _ _ _ _ N _ _ _
football jacket	anger idea

Clue: A _ _ _ _ _ _ _ _ _	Clue: V _ _ _
humorous mysterious	write think

Write six sentences using some of your words.

Quiz 2

. . . .

What kind of word am I?

Add as many as you can to each list.

A _ _ _ _ _ of P _ _ _ _	A _ _ _ _ _ of T _ _ _	A _ _ _ _ _ of M _ _ _ _ _
above	already	anxiously
below	meanwhile	noisily
1		
2		
3		
4		
5		
6		
7		
8		
9		
10		
11		
12		
13		
14		

Write six sentences using some of your words.

_____

_____

_____

_____

_____

Assessment checklist

Name	Term		
	1	2	3
Can understand and use the following terminology:			
Subject			
Object			
Active			
Passive			
Synonym			
Antonym			
Ellipsis			
Hyphen			
Colon			
Semi-colon			
Bullet points			
Understands and is able to:			
Use hyphens to avoid ambiguity			
Use ellipses to show missing text, that something is continued or to add tension			
Use semi-colons instead of a conjunction			
Use bullet points to list information			
Use semi-colons to punctuate complex lists			
Use dashes, semi-colons and colons to join two independent clauses			
Identify the subject and object in a sentence			
Identify and use active and passive voice			
Use synonyms in their writing			
Use antonyms in their writing			
Identify modal verbs and know when they are used			
Identify the subjunctive mood			
Use formal and informal language and understand when each is used			
Identify homonyms, homophones and homographs			
Avoid using double negatives in their writing			
Use similes			
Use metaphors			
Find the base word			
Use layout devices such as headings, sub-headings, columns, bullet points and tables to organise text			
Use a range of linking devices to provide cohesion between paragraphs			

Answers

And a semi-colon is … (pg 9)
He was tired out; he'd never run so fast.
My teacher is good; I have to listen carefully.
We play football in winter; we play cricket in summer.
She wanted to visit her Nan; she had no bus fare.

More semi-colons (pg 11)
For the trip, Emma has brought her rucksack full of games to play; two sets of pyjamas; her mum's photograph; six different kinds of biscuit and a teddy bear with only one eye.
In the dressing-up box were hats of all kinds and shapes; jackets with buttons and zips; so many shoes you wouldn't believe; masks of every animal you can think of; enough tops and trousers for the whole class.

Bullet points with semi-colons (pg 12)
Punctuation marks children might use: full stop, comma, question mark, exclamation mark, colon, semi-colon, dash, hyphen etc.

Verb voice (pg 20)
A big, hairy spider was pounced on by my dog./My dog pounced on a big hairy spider.
The activities were all chosen by the children in the group./The group of children all chose the activities.
The flowers were all picked by my Nan./My Nan picked all the flowers.
Six goals were scored by Henry./Henry scored six goals.
The cat was frightened by the frog./The frog frightened the cat.
Ten stickers were awarded to Kevin./Kevin was awarded ten stickers.

Verb voice again (pg 21)
Tony fixed the car./The car was fixed by Tony.
Rain stopped the carnival parade./The carnival parade was stopped by rain.
The noise came from under a bush./From under the bush came a noise. Humpty Dumpty fell off the wall./Off the wall fell Humpty Dumpty.
The chicken walked across the road./Across the road walked the chicken.
Jenna stood by the table./By the table stood Jenna.The dog gobbled up the sausages./The sausages were gobbled up by the dog.

The aliens stepped out of the UFO./Out of the UFO stepped the aliens.
The squirrel ran across the fence./Across the fence ran the squirrel.

Words that help your writing (pg 23)

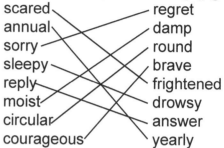

scared — frightened
annual — yearly
sorry — regret
sleepy — drowsy
reply — answer
moist — damp
circular — round
courageous — brave

Base words (pg 24)
For example:
appear: <u>dis</u>appear<u>ance</u>
respect: <u>dis</u>respect<u>ful</u>
correct: <u>in</u>correct<u>ness</u>
honest: <u>dis</u>honest<u>y</u>
certain: <u>un</u>certain<u>ty</u>
pleasant: <u>un</u>pleasant<u>ness</u>
construct: <u>re</u>construc<u>tion</u>
joy: <u>en</u>joy<u>able</u>

un	employ	ment
un	certain	ty
dis	respect	ful
re	construct	ion
un	pleasant	ness
dis	honour	able
im	prison	ment
en	joy	able
in	formal	ly
in	correct	ly
re	appear	ing

Compound words (pg 25)
cheesebrow = cheeseburger
everyache = everyday
homeball = homework
footshake = football
handfly = handshake
toothwork = toothache
eyeburger = eyebrow
butterday = butterfly

Does it mean the same? (pg 26)
coast: beach, seaside, shoreline
daring: bold, fearless, brave

Brilliant Activities for Grammar and Punctuation, Year 6
© Irene Yates and Brilliant Publications

jump: leap, hop, bound, spring
honest: truthful, sincere, frank, open, genuine
hot: boiling, roasting, blistering,
good: nice, fine, fit, talented, tip-top

Synonym word search (pg 27)

f	l	a	v	o	u	r	d	e	p
s	a	b	e	c	l	x	p	m	e
n	r	d	l	l	a	d	t	t	c
r	g	s	i	c	k	a	i	i	l
g	e	a	p	p	u	o	n	p	a
e	m	p	t	y	c	f	y	u	p
x	f	l	a	o	s	t	i	g	n
y	e	x	i	t	o	u	b	x	s
e	m	p	s	t	r	a	n	g	e

big/large, ancient/old, small/tiny, mend/fix,
taste/flavour, hollow/empty, ill/sick, applaud/
clap, odd/strange, way out/exit

Does it mean the opposite? (pg 28)

storm/calm, quick/slow, hurry/dawdle, silence/
noisy, enormous/tiny, entertain/bore, entrance/
exit, enter/leave, universal/only, tidiness/
messiness

Antonym word search (pg 29)

f	s	m	i	l	e	c	r	t	i
o	m	t	q	u	t	r	o	i	m
f	q	u	i	e	t	y	g	l	e
a	t	h	e	g	c	j	o	m	d
k	y	q	u	o	h	y	g	e	u
e	n	o	i	f	e	t	h	a	e
t	i	m	i	d	a	s	e	n	a
b	r	a	c	k	p	v	y	l	u
e	x	p	e	l	i	g	h	t	h

hot/cold, expensive/cheap, loose/tight, heavy/
light, real/fake, noisy/quiet, generous/mean,
frown/smile, laugh/cry, brave/timid.

Negative modal verbs (pg 32)

You mightn't be lucky and win.
She wouldn't believe me.
I couldn't eat an elephant.
I shouldn't be late for school.
They won't catch cold in the rain. (Watch out!)
He mightn't be on time.
I may not watch the programme.
They mustn't hurry.
They can't dance and sing.
I shall be there.
I should have bothered.
She might be early.
He will like it.

The subjunctive (pg 33)

If it were to rain we'd postpone the match.
If wishes and dreams were to come true you'd
be OK.
If wild cats were as tame as domestic cats –
they'd be safe.
If your dog were trained properly I'd let it in.
If those children were well behaved I'd enjoy
being with them.
If Grandad were to wear a hat it'd keep his
head warm.

Homonyms (pg 39)

Homographs: bark, box, well.
Homophones: pear/pair, hare/hair, lead/led,
flower/flour, poor/pour.

Don't do this! (pg 40)

She didn't want anything.
They couldn't play any games.
There wasn't any left.
That old man doesn't like anybody.
We never went anywhere.
She doesn't want any sandwiches.
He doesn't know anything.
We've never had any of these games.

Anagrams (pg 41)

seal/sale, plum/lump, rose/sore, mane/name,
rats/star, last/salt, mate/team, same/seam,
verse/sever, garden/danger/gander
aals/alas, aenprrt//partner, abdn/band, aenprtt/
pattern, achir/chair, aaccdeim/academic,
achls/clash, aaccertu/accurate,
aadfir/afraid, aadlns/sandal.

Similes (pg 42)

as cunning as a <u>fox</u>
as proud as a <u>peacock</u>
as flat as a <u>pancake</u>
as old as the <u>hills</u>
as fresh as a <u>daisy</u>
as safe as <u>houses</u>
as quick as <u>lightning</u>
as sweet as <u>sugar</u>
as black as <u>coal</u>
as busy as a <u>bee</u>

Quiz 1 (pg 47)

Common Noun, Abstract Noun, Adjective,
Verb.

Quiz 2 (pg 48)

Adverb of Place, Adverb of Time, Adverb of
Manner.

Lightning Source UK Ltd.
Milton Keynes UK
UKOW07f2313290416

273260UK00003B/20/P